YELLOWSTONE

NATIONAL PARK

FOR THE BENEFIT AND
ENJOYMENT OF THE PEOPLE

YELLOWSTONE
NATIONAL
PARK

YELLOWSTONE
NATIONAL PARK

NATIONAL PARKS AND
CONSERVATION ASSOCIATION

———

By David Dunbar
Photography by Jerry Pavia

A TINY FOLIO™
Abbeville Press · Publishers
New York · London · Paris

EDITOR: Susan Costello
DESIGNER: Celia Fuller
PRODUCTION EDITOR: Abigail Asher
PRODUCTION MANAGER: Lou Bilka
MAPS: Guenter Vollath
CONSULTANT: Ken Sinay, Director, Northern Rockies Natural History Service

FRONT COVER: The Grand Canyon of the Yellowstone
BACK COVER: Rocky Mountain Bull Elk in velvet • SPINE: Old Faithful

To the memory of my sister, Geraldine (1948–1991).

*I'd like to thank Jim Pena and Nick Tucker for spending time with me in
Yellowstone chasing the light and dancing in it once we caught it.*
JERRY PAVIA

FIRST EDITION
2 4 6 8 10 9 7 5 3 1

Library of Congress Cataloging-in-Publication Data
Caulfield, Patricia.
Everglades National Park/National Parks and Conservation
Association ; photographs by Patricia Caulfield ; text by Ted Levin.
p. cm. — (A tiny folio)
Includes index.
ISBN 1-55859-827-8
1. Everglades National Park (Fla.) 2. Everglades National Park (Fla.)—Pictorial
works. 3. Natural history—Florida—Everglades National Park. 4. Natural history—Florida—Everglades National Park—Pictorial works. I. Levin, Ted, 1948– .
II. National Parks and Conservation Association. III. Title. IV. Series: Tiny folios.
F317.E9C38 1995
917. 59'390463—dc20   94-46988

CONTENTS

PREFACE

The world's first and foremost park, Yellowstone is a wondrous place boasting geological, ecological, and scenic splendor.

When explorers first came upon what is now Yellowstone, it must have amazed them more than anything they had seen across our vast continent. With its 10,000 geysers and hot springs, in addition to spectacular lakes, waterfalls, rivers, and canyons, Yellowstone is one of the most awe-inspiring places on Earth. And enough people were overwhelmed by it that, at the end of a great century in the history of mankind—a century in which a free nation's economic opportunity, development, and human rights all came together—the idea of a national park was born.

Established in 1872, Yellowstone was the first national park in the world. Since then, more than 365 other park units have been created in the U.S. National Park System, and some 120 other nations have modeled their park systems on ours, setting aside their most superlative natural and cultural resources. Yellowstone set the standard not only for our own park system, but for parks worldwide.

Now, more than a century later, Yellowstone National Park is threatened by mining, logging, and oil drilling operations just outside its borders. A proposed nearby gold mine, for example, would endanger three major watersheds of the Yellowstone River, imperil water quality within the park, and destroy habitat for grizzly bears and other wildlife. The National Parks and Conservation Association is working to forestall this and other developments that threaten to degrade Yellowstone's famed wilderness character.

We, as Americans, must recognize that Yellowstone is both a treasure and a symbol, a cherished part of our national heritage and a model for the world. Above all, we must commit ourselves to defending it from harm.

This book conveys Yellowstone's glorious beauty and inspirational values. We hope it will inspire you to learn about the world's first national park and help you understand its legacy.

PAUL C. PRITCHARD
President, National Parks and
Conservation Association

INTRODUCTION

The reports of explorers and trappers that trickled back east beginning in the early 1800s about a strange region beyond the Missouri River must have seemed like the ravings of mountain men gone mad. The earth seethed with scalding vapors, it was said. Geysers gushed skyward. Mud bubbled in sulfurous caldrons. Hot springs steamed in rainbow hues. Walking among them, wrote a nineteenth-century trapper, "one feels that in a moment he may break through and be lost in a species of hell."

By the 1860s the area's seemingly fanciful natural wonders had been well documented. Early conservationists began lobbying the federal government to protect Yellowstone's "remarkable curiosities" and "beautiful decorations," as one contemporary magazine article described them, from private or commercial exploitation. In response, President Ulysses S.

Old Faithful, the park's best-known geyser.

Grant signed a bill on March 1, 1872, establishing Yellowstone National Park, to be "set apart as a public park or pleasuring-ground for the benefit and enjoyment of the people." The nation's—and the world's—first national park was born.

Although it shelters many natural marvels, Yellowstone is perhaps best known as a geological park, still in the throes of creation. Yellowstone lies over a hot spot—a place where molten rock, or magma, rises in a column called a thermal plume from deep within the earth's mantle. Yellowstone's plume feeds a magma dome only 11,000 feet (3.3 km) below the surface. This fiery reservoir is some 30 miles (48 km) across and extends at least 50 miles (80 km) into the earth.

The dome has burst in at least three main explosions: 2 million years ago, 1.2 million years ago, and again some 600,000 years ago. The third cataclysm hurled skyward a thousand times more material than the 1980 Mount St. Helens eruption, catapulting tons of hot pumice, ash, rock, and debris more than 30 miles (48 km) into the atmosphere. Rock from this explosion landed as far away as Kansas and Nebraska.

Once the magma chamber burst for the third time, its roof collapsed to form a crater, or caldera, more than a mile (1.6 km) deep and 50 miles (80 km) across. Over the next 500,000 years, subsequent lava flows nearly filled the caldera, erasing all but the fragmented mountains that outline parts of its rim. In fact, the caldera was not clearly recognized until the 1960s, when scientists mapped it from the air. In and around the caldera, which now forms the central part of the park, are ten thousand thermal features, fueled by the molten rock that has refilled the subterranean magma chamber.

Water from snow and rain seeps through the caldera's porous lava to be heated by the magma below, which reaches temperatures of more than 450°F (230°C). If unobstructed, the resulting steam rises and escapes through vents called fumaroles, such as those that dot the Norris Geyser Basin (pages 88–93). If it reaches the surface as a trickle of acidic water instead, the clayish soil bubbles like a muddy stew. The most impressive mud pot is Mud Volcano (pages 82–85) along the Yellowstone River just north of Yellowstone Lake.

Hot springs and geysers occur where hot water finds a route to the surface by moving slowly through a maze of cracks and fissures. With no place to escape, the water becomes superheated under pressure, sometimes reaching triple its aboveground boiling point. Finally, expanding steam bubbles push the water through any available vent to the surface. Wide openings allow water and steam to well up in pools of exquisite beauty, such as Grand Prismatic Spring (pages 97, 114) in the Midway Geyser Basin north of Old Faithful.

Constricted openings force water and steam to shoot up intermittently in three hundred or so active geysers. (One hundred and thirty active geysers are found within a mile of Old Faithful in the Upper Geyser Basin—a quarter of the world's total.) Steamboat Geyser (page 88) in the Norris Basin once set a world record by sending scalding water 400 feet (120 m) into the air, but Steamboat's usual height is about 300 feet (90 m). Great Fountain Geyser in the Lower Geyser Basin to the south sometimes reaches 200 feet (60 m). Old Faithful (pages 10, 120) tops out at about 180 feet (54 m), but makes up for its lack of height with regularity—erupting every 75 minutes or so.

The Yellowstone Caldera is bracketed on the west by the Gallatin Range and on the east by the Absarokas. Broad, rumpled plateaus flatten the landscape throughout the park: the Blacktail Deer Plateau in the north, the Mirror Plateau in the northeast, the Madison

Plateau in the west, and the Pitchstone and Two Ocean Plateaus in the south.

Ice, not fire, produced the park's most spectacular nonthermal feature, the Grand Canyon of the Yellowstone (pages 22, 72–77). When Pleistocene glaciers waned some twelve thousand years ago, meltwater cut through soft layers of rhyolite lava to form a gorge some 20 miles (32 km) long, up to 4,000 feet (1,200 m) wide, and as much as 1,500 feet (460 m) deep. The park's superheated plumbing did play a role, though, in the Grand Canyon's present appearance. It cooked the gorge's rhyolite walls into a gaudy palette of red, brown, white, orange, and the distinctive yellow that gave the park its name.

At the head of the canyon, Upper Falls plunges 109 feet (33.2 m) into a rocky amphitheater. The river roils downstream for half a mile, then at Lower Falls (page 73) bursts from between narrowing walls in a curtain of white water that spills 308 feet (93.9 m). The view of the cataract from Artist Point (page 74) on the South Rim of the canyon is one of the most sublime sights on the continent.

Yellowstone's thermal basins, canyonlands, plateaus, high-country meadows, and lodgepole pine forests support thriving populations of wildlife. Some sixty species of mammals are found here, from the tiniest shrews and voles scuttling about dead leaves and meadow grasses to the great, dish-faced grizzly bear, at half a ton the largest land-dwelling carnivore south of Alaska.

The park's estimated two hundred grizzlies are lords of the backcountry, ranging unchallenged from river valleys to subalpine meadows. Some of the best bear habitat is in the Washburn Range in north-central Yellowstone, near Fishing Bridge (page 136) on the north shore of Yellowstone Lake, and in the 12,000 acres (4,900 hectares) of open meadow within the Pelican Creek drainage northeast of Yellowstone Lake.

Black bears, lynx, and bobcat—all elusive and seldom seen—roam dark forest galleries in remote reaches of the park. Nimble-footed bighorn sheep and mountain goats find safety and food on mountain heights. Mule deer wander the slopes, moose browse on succulent water plants along the margins of lakes and rivers and pronghorn antelope graze sagebrush flats in the north. Some three thousand free-ranging bison in three herds wander throughout the park.

Yellowstone has one of the world's largest populations of elk—in summer, more than thirty thousand animals in eight herds. During warm weather, most of the elk seek cool, high pastures; a few stay behind to forage on bottomland grasses, rewarding wildlife watchers. In late October and early November, as winter snows begin to accumulate, most of the elk migrate south to their winter haven in the National Elk Refuge near Jackson, Wyoming.

In Yellowstone's early years, public enjoyment usually took precedence over preservation. That meant, among other things, ensuring that the park's "bad" animals (wolves, cougars, and coyotes) didn't menace the "good" animals (elk, bighorn sheep, mule deer, and pronghorn). Between 1904 and 1935, hunters and trappers killed 121 mountain lions, 4,352 coyotes, and 136 gray wolves.

Today, about twenty mountain lions form a resident population in the Northern Range. The adaptable coyote was never seriously threatened. Wolves, however, were probably extirpated locally by the 1940s. Then, in 1995, after dozens of studies and prolonged court battles between conservationists and ranchers who feared the predators would decimate cattle herds, 150 gray wolves from Alberta, Canada, were released in the park. It will take years to determine whether the

1 MAMMOTH REGION
2 ROOSEVELT REGION
3 CANYON REGION
4 GEYSER REGION
5 LAKE REGION

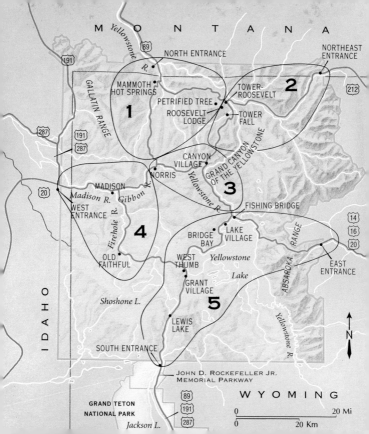

A world of wonders awaits within Yellowstone, a wild but fragile realm of grizzlies, bison, elk, geysers, hot springs, pyramid peaks, lodgepole forests, petrified forests, quaking aspens, and earthquakes.

As shown on the map on pages 18–19, the park may be divided into five regions for ease of exploration. The Mammoth Region (1) in the northwest corner of Yellowstone includes Mammoth Hot Springs and the Blacktail Deer Plateau, home to pronghorns and abundant other animals. The Roosevelt Region (2) in the northeast contains the wildlife-rich Lamar Valley and bizarre petrified forests along Specimen Ridge.

The main attraction of the Canyon Region (3) is the Grand Canyon of the Yellowstone. The Norris Geyser Basin also amazes with mud pots, geysers, and hot springs. The Geyser Region (4) in the southwest is home to Old Faithful, the park's most famous feature. Along the Firehole River are the massive geyserite battlements of Castle Geyser, the ground-shaking spurts of the Giantess and the transparent rich blues of the Sapphire Pool hot spring.

North America's largest mountain lake is the centerpiece of the Lake Region (5) in the southeast. Yellowstone Lake is flanked by a trio of smaller alpine lakes—Shoshone, Lewis, and Heart.

relocation has been successful.

The broad, flat delta where the Yellowstone River flows into the Southeast Arm of Yellowstone Lake is a rich habitat for gadwalls, wigeons, goldeneyes, Canada geese, loons, ospreys, harriers, and other bird life. White pelicans nest in the Southeast Arm on two tiny mounds of sand and volcanic boulders called the Molly Islands. It is the only white pelican nesting colony in America's national parks.

The tremendous diversity of natural wonders crowded into the 3,472 square miles (8,992 km²) of the largest park in the contiguous United States provokes awe in 3 million visitors a year. Five entrances spaced around the park's perimeter funnel motorists onto a central figure eight called the Grand Loop Road, which provides access to Yellowstone's major attractions.

Heavy summer use and frequent wildlife sightings often clog the Grand Loop Road with urban-style traffic jams. Hikers and trail riders, however, only have to venture a short distance from pavement and other works of humankind to encounter the magnificent wilderness that astonished the mountain men.

SCENIC TOURS

The following portfolios introduce some of the grandest scenery on earth. The photographs are organized into five touring regions, each accompanied by a map that shows roads and services areas and pinpoints natural wonders, scenic lookouts, and other points of interest.

Tour 1 covers the Mammoth Region in the northwest corner of the park. The centerpiece is Mammoth Hot Springs, which flows over towering terraces of porcelain-like travertine. Most of the park is underlain with lava, but at Mammoth hot water rises through limestone. The water's cargo of dissolved calcium carbonate settles out to become the building material for Mammoth's elaborate architecture.

Other attractions include the rugged Gallatin Range, the Gardner River, and the glassy black face of Obsidian Cliff, where Indians used to gather the brittle

---

The park's most spectacular vista: the Grand Canyon of the Yellowstone from Inspiration Point near Canyon Village.

volcanic glass prized for making arrowheads and tools. The road winds high above the Yellowstone River on the Blacktail Deer Plateau, a pronghorn's delight of grassy valleys and sagebrush flats.

A highlight of Tour 2, the Roosevelt Region, is the world's largest fossil forest. Trees that grew 50 million years ago—pine, spruce, fir, aspen, willow, and cottonwood—still stand on some twenty-four square miles (62 km) of Specimen Ridge. Lava and volcanic ash buried the forests, in time turning the wood to stone. In one area, twenty-seven successive forests were interred, one above the other.

Also in the region is the 10,243-foot (3,073 m) Mount Washburn, part of a 50-million-year-old volcano that lost much of its bulk when it collapsed some 600,000 years ago to form the Great Yellowstone Caldera. Just south, the road crosses Dunraven Pass, another piece of the northern rim of the caldera.

Tour 3, the Canyon Region in the heart of the park, includes scenic lookouts with spectacular views of the Grand Canyon of the Yellowstone and Upper and Lower Falls. Many regard the view from Artist Point looking up-canyon to 308-foot (93.9 m) Lower Falls to be the park's most spectacular vista. The touring region also takes in Mud Volcano and the Norris Geyser Basin, one of the hottest and most active geyser basins in the world. The thermal features bubble, spurt, and steam in a barren moonscape quite unlike anything else in the park.

In Tour 4, the Geyser Region, visitors pass an extraordinary string of thermal features along the Firehole River north to the Madison River. Despite the crowds in summer, Old Faithful is a must-see on most people's itinerary. Nearby Biscuit Basin, on the west side of the Firehole River, offers greater solitude. At the Midway Basin, the Excelsior Geyser Crater pours hundreds of gallons of hot water each minute into the Firehole. Before Excelsior blew out its plumbing in 1888, its eruptions were 300 feet (90 m) high.

Tour 5, the Lake Region of the southeast corner, features Yellowstone Lake, a vast body of high-altitude water that is home to a huge population of cutthroat trout. In thermal areas along the shore, steam vents or gas fumaroles in the lake floor cause the usually frigid water to bubble. In the West Thumb area, which occupies the crater of what was once a small volcano, subterranean magma turns mud boiling hot about three feet (1 m) below the lake bottom.

TOUR 1 MAMMOTH REGION

From the park's North Entrance, drive south on US Highway 89 along the Gardner River to Mammoth Hot Springs. Continue south past Obsidian Cliff to Nymph Lake, then return north.

At Mammoth, drive east on U.S. Highway 212 across the Blacktail Deer Plateau, paralleling the Yellowstone River. The one-way, seven-mile (11 km) Blacktail Plateau Drive branches off the highway to follow a section of the Bannock Trail, a route used until the 1880s by Idaho's Bannock Indians to reach bison herds on the plains northeast of Yellowstone. Return to Highway 212 and take a spur road to the Petrified Tree, the only fossilized tree in the park accessible by car. The tour ends at the Tower-Roosevelt Junction.

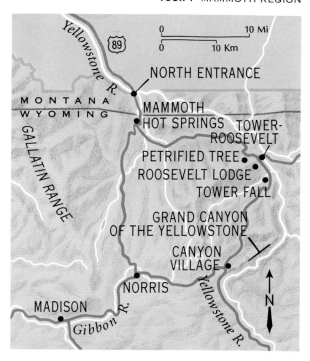

ABOVE. The Gardner River, named after a fur trapper,
Johnson Gardner, flowing through open country.
PAGES 28–29. The Mammoth Hot Springs area, located near
the North Entrance to the park.

Cottonwoods in fall color alongside the Gardner River.

Above. Deer, elk, bighorn sheep, and other wildlife are often seen on the lower slopes of 7,841-foot (2,390 m) Mount Everts. **Opposite.** Liberty Cap at Mammoth Hot Springs was named after the caps worn by patriots during the Revolutionary War.

Jupiter Terrace, Mammoth Hot Springs.

Jupiter Spring, Mammoth Hot Springs.

ABOVE. At Mammoth Terraces hot water rises up through soluble limestone and leaves behind deposits of a mineral called travertine.
OPPOSITE. Opal Terrace, Mammoth Hot Springs.

Devil's Thumb, Mammoth Hot Springs.

Cupid Spring, Upper Terrace Area, Mammoth Hot Springs.

Bunsen Peak, which reaches an elevation of 8,564 feet
(2,610 m), is named in honor of Robert Bunsen, inventor
of the Bunsen burner.

Rustic Falls at the Golden Gate, south of
Mammoth Hot Springs.

Above. Indian Creek with a view of Sheepeater Cliff.
Pages 42–43. Swan Lake with Antler Peak in the distance.

Sheepeater Cliff was named after the Sheepeater Indians,
who specialized in hunting bighorns.

ABOVE. Roaring Mountain.
OPPOSITE. Twin Lakes.

Near Blacktail Ponds.

Floating Island Lake.

ABOVE. A petrified tree, Specimen Ridge.
OPPOSITE. Burnt lodgepole pine forest near a petrified tree.

TOUR 2 ROOSEVELT REGION

From Tower-Roosevelt, follow Highway 212 through the Lamar Valley, then along Soda Butte Creek to the Northeast Entrance. Return west to Tower-Roosevelt, then drive south on the Grand Loop Road. Just south of 132-foot (40 m)-high Tower Fall, the road sweeps around the Mae West Curve above the Antelope Creek Valley as it climbs along the west slope of Mount Washburn. The tour ends just south of Washburn in Dunraven Pass, at 8,859 feet (2,700 m) the highest roadway elevation in the park.

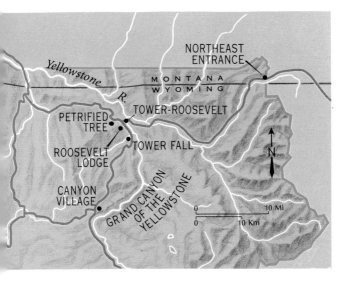

NORTHEAST
ENTRANCE

Yellowstone

M O N T A N A
W Y O M I N G

R. TOWER-ROOSEVELT

PETRIFIED
TREE

TOWER FALL

ROOSEVELT
LODGE

N

CANYON
VILLAGE

GRAND CANYON
OF THE
YELLOWSTONE

0   10 Mi
0   10 Km

ABOVE. Tower Fall.
OPPOSITE. Geyser Basin with the Tetons in the distance.

A pond near Slough Creek. Specimen Ridge, in the
background, contains the world's largest fossil forest.

Between Tower Fall and Slough Creek in autumn.

A dramatic skyline over the Lamar Valley.

ABOVE. Sunset over a pond in the Lamar Valley.
PAGES 60–61. Basalt along canyon walls at Calcite Springs.

PAGES 62–63 AND ABOVE. The Yellowstone River at
Calcite Springs.
OPPOSITE. Tower Fall, a 132-foot (40 m) cascade, is one of the
park's most visited attractions.

PAGES 66–67: Mount Washburn (10,243 feet; 3,122 m) is composed mostly of angular chunks of rock embedded in a matrix of undifferentiated sedimentary, igneous, and metamorphic rock.

Above. Burnt forest on the slopes of Mount Washburn.
Opposite. Snow dusts the trees on Dunraven Pass, which
was named after the Earl of Dunraven, who visited the
park in 1874.

TOUR 3 CANYON REGION

Tour 3 begins at Dunraven Pass and heads south to the Canyon Village area. Continue past Canyon Village and take the one-way loop on the North Rim of the Grand Canyon of the Yellowstone. Stop at Grandview Point for a distant look at the canyon and at Lookout Point for views of the Lower Falls.

At the end of the loop, turn left at the stop sign, head south, then turn left again at the sign for "Grand Canyon Artist Point." Cross the Yellowstone River to the South Rim. Take the first left, into the Uncle Tom's Trail parking lot, for a closer look at the Upper Falls. Continue down the road to Artist Point for the classic view of the Lower Falls.

After touring the canyon, drive south along the Yellowstone River to the Mud Volcano area, then backtrack north to Canyon Village. Go west past the exit of the Virginia Cascade Drive, then take the next left at the entrance of this exciting one-way road, which narrows as it climbs above the falls.

Continue west to the Norris Geyser Basin. Just north of Norris Junction, the National Park Ranger Museum holds exhibits on the history of the National Park Service. The tour ends a few miles west at Beryl Spring.

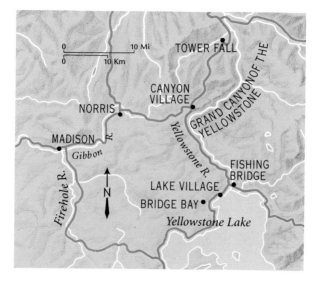

The Grand Canyon of the Yellowstone.

At 308 feet (93.9 m), the Lower Falls in the Grand Canyon of the Yellowstone are almost twice as high as Niagara Falls.

Above. For twenty miles (32 km) the Yellowstone River flows
through the Grand Canyon of the Yellowstone.
Opposite. The Grand Canyon of the Yellowstone from
Artist Point.

Above. The Yellowstone River winding through the Grand
Canyon of the Yellowstone.
Opposite. The Yellowstone River from Inspiration Point.
A rim trail leads to other breathtaking vistas at Grandview
Point and Lookout Point.

Pages 78–79 and Above. The Yellowstone River meanders through Hayden Valley, a mecca for bison, bear, elk, deer, and waterfowl.

The Yellowstone River in the Hayden Valley northwest of
Yellowstone Lake.

A thermal pool near Mud Volcano.

Mud Caldron at Mud Volcano, where springs occasionally
hurl large chunks of mud dozens of feet into the air.

Above. A bison on the edge of Black Dragon's Caldron
at Mud Volcano.
Opposite. Dragon Mouth Spring at Mud Volcano.

    In early summer cutthroat trout leap through Le Hardy
Rapids to reach Clear Creek and other spawning streams.

Virginia Cascade.

Irregular in its eruptions and dormant for long periods of time, Steamboat Geyser in the Norris Geyser Basin is the world's tallest geyser, erupting in a column of scalding water nearly 300 feet (120 m) high.

Like all geysers in the Norris Basin, Echinus Geyser spouts
acidic water. Depending on the wind, Echinus may spray
its vinegary plume on visitors watching from the
viewing platform.

Porcelain Basin, Norris Geyser Basin.

Above. Porcelain Terrace Springs, Norris Geyser Basin.
Pages 92–93. Big Whirligig Geyser, Norris Geyser Basin.

TOUR 4 GEYSER REGION

From Beryl Spring, drive west on US Highway 20 along the Gibbon River. At Gibbon Falls the river spills over the lip of the ancient Yellowstone Caldera. There are spectacular views from here of burned forest on high, flat volcanic plateaus. Continue past Madison to the West Entrance, then backtrack Madison.

Just south of the junction, the scenic one-way Firehole Canyon Drive winds two miles (3.2 km) between steep rhyolite cliffs along the Firehole River. Farther south, opposite the Fountain Paint Pot, the Firehole Lake Drive branches off the main road to pass the Great Fountain Geyser. Continuing south back on the main road, a series of thermal areas reaches its apex at Old Faithful, where the route ends.

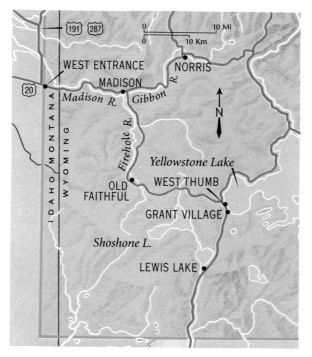

Madison River near the park's western boundary.

Grand Prismatic Spring, Yellowstone's largest hot spring
at 370 feet (110 m) in diameter.

ABOVE. Beryl Spring.
OPPOSITE. A Rocky Mountain bull elk resting in Gibbon
Meadow, a favorite grazing area.

Above. A subalpine fir growing close to a canyon wall near Gibbon Falls.
Opposite. Gibbon Falls.

ABOVE. Firehole Falls on the Firehole River.
OPPOSITE. Firehole River.

Trumpeter swans with young.

Rocky Mountain cow elk with calf near the Madison River.

Above. Lupines brighten park meadows in summer.
Opposite. A short hike from the end of Fountain Flat Drive
leads to 200-foot (60 m) Fairy Falls.

ABOVE. The mud in Fountain Paint Pot is composed of clay
and particles of silica.
OPPOSITE. Clepsydra Geyser, Fountain Paint Pot
thermal area.

109

Surprise Pool along Firehole Lake Drive.

White Dome Geyser along Firehole Lake Drive, which shoots water thirty feet (9.2 m) into the air, has an opening only four inches (10 cm) wide.

ABOVE. Opal Pool, Midway Geyser Basin.
OPPOSITE. Frost rims the banks of a creek while thermal
areas steam in the background along Firehole Lake Drive.

ABOVE. Grand Prismatic Spring, Midway Geyser Basin.
OPPOSITE. The Firehole River with steam rising from the
Midway Geyser Basin in the background.

Sapphire Pool, Biscuit Basin.

Black Opal Spring, Biscuit Basin.

Iron Spring Creek, Black Sand Basin.

Spouter Geyser, Black Sand Basin.

ABOVE. Beauty Pool in the Old Faithful area is renowned for its azure water.

OPPOSITE. Old Faithful, which earns its name every hour or so, has not missed a performance since explorers first observed the geyser more than 120 years ago.

ABOVE. Eruptions of Grotto Geyser in the Old Faithful area rise as high as ten feet (3 m) and last as long as ten hours.
OPPOSITE. Riverside Geyser, in the Old Faithful area.

The resemblance to its namesake's shape and color make Morning Glory Pool in the Old Faithful area one of the park's most beautiful thermal features.

TOUR 5 LAKE REGION

This driving tour starts in the Old Faithful area and goes east to the vast bay on Yellowstone Lake called the West Thumb. The route then continues along the northern shore of the lake. Just south of Bridge Bay, the main road heads slightly inland. Follow Gull Point Drive to continue along the shoreline.

The route passes Lake Village and Fishing Bridge, both with extensive visitor facilities, then curves around the lake's eastern shore before scaling Sylvan Pass (8,530 ft.; 2,600 m) en route to the East Entrance of the park.

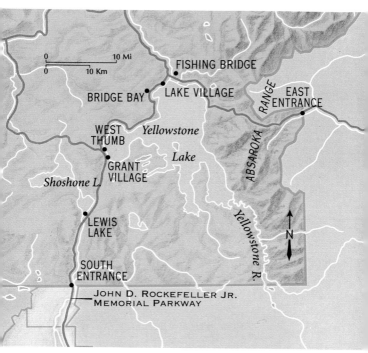

ABOVE. Yellowstone River entering Yellowstone Lake.
OPPOSITE. Yellowstone Lake is one of the largest alpine lakes in the world, with a shoreline of 110 miles (177 km).

ABOVE. The waters of Isa Lake, perched on the Continental
Divide just southeast of Old Faithful, drain both
east and west.
OPPOSITE. Kepler Cascade.

ABOVE. Isa Lake in late fall.
OPPOSITE. Frigid Yellowstone Lake, shown here from West
Thumb, has an average summer temperature of 45°F (7°C).

ABOVE. Blue Funnel Spring, West Thumb Geyser Basin.
OPPOSITE. Thumb Paint Pots, West Thumb Geyser Basin.

Fishing Bridge, where the Yellowstone River flows out
of Yellowstone Lake.

The meeting of Pelican Creek and Yellowstone Lake, with the Absaroka Range's volcanic peaks in the distance.

Indian Pond, Pelican Valley.

Bison gather at a thermal area at Mary Bay on the north-eastern shore of Yellowstone Lake.

ABOVE. American globeflowers near Sylvan Lake.
OPPOSITE. Yellowstone Lake from Steamboat Point.

Burnt lodgepole forest near Lewis Lake.

Yellowstone Lake from Lake Butte.

Sylvan Lake.

Burnt lodgepole forest near Lewis Lake.

WILDLIFE

Yellowstone shelters the greatest concentration of mammals in the Lower Forty-eight, as well as large populations of shorebirds, waterfowl, and perching birds. The park is inhabited by nearly every animal species that was here when explorers first ventured west, including the recently reintroduced gray wolf. For many, the sighting of a bison or bald eagle is the thrill of a lifetime, a powerful evocation of the Old West: vast stretches of wilderness teeming with wildlife.

Yellowstone's remarkable fauna is available for viewing from nearly any vantage point along the park's highways and trails. River valleys provide some of the best opportunities to see wildlife. Moose and bison are sighted most of the year feeding on marshy growths and meadows along the meandering Yellowstone River in the Hayden Valley north of Yellowstone Lake. Across the river from the road, grizzlies are sometimes seen.

Bison along the Yellowstone River.

A bald eagle fishing.

An important breeding ground for waterfowl and other birds is the delta of the Yellowstone River where it flows into the Southeast Arm of Yellowstone Lake. The delta is accessible only by boat or canoe. Northeast of the lake, white pelicans frequent the lush meadows of Pelican Valley, which is also a favorite grizzly habitat. Flocks of sandhill cranes feed along the marshy banks of the Firehole River, poking with daggerlike beaks for roots of marsh plants and occasionally jabbing for frogs or fish.

Even winter visitors are rewarded with abundant animal sightings. The Northern Range, warmer and drier than the park interior, is an important wintering ground for large mammals. Warm water flowing from geyser basins keeps the Firehole River open all winter for ducks and geese.

The park's tiniest organisms, algae and bacteria, combine with minerals to turn thermal pools into steaming palettes. The colors are a guide to water temperature. Most of the algae and bacteria form green clumps in water that ranges from 122°F to 140°F (50–60°C). In hotter water, green organisms give way to orange, then yellow. Around the edges of the pool, depending on water temperature and acidity, algae add bands of yellow, lime green, orange, brown, and purple.

A pika carrying plant cuttings to its nest.

A snowshoe hare can leap up to twelve feet (3.7 m).

ABOVE. The yellow-bellied marmot fattens up on green vege-
tation, then hibernates from late August to early spring.
OPPOSITE. The Uinta ground squirrel's hibernation lasts
six to seven months.

ABOVE. Yellow-pine chipmunks are often seen around lodgepole pines.
OPPOSITE. This red squirrel lives in an aspen cavity hollowed out by a flicker.

ABOVE. A muskrat, shown here feeding on grass, has the same habitat as a beaver.
OPPOSITE. A beaver cuts an aspen for food.

ABOVE. A coyote in freshly fallen snow.
PAGES 158–59. A porcupine with its young.

A red fox in melting ice on a frozen lake.

ABOVE. Black bear cubs climbing.
PAGES 162–63. A black bear at the Gardner River, where sightings are frequent.

Black bear sow and her brood of older cubs.

The grizzly bear: an endangered, powerful, and
unpredictable omnivore.

Grizzly sow with cub.

ABOVE. An ermine, waiting to pounce on prey, may weigh as
little as two ounces, yet it brings down animals far larger
than itself, including squirrels and rabbits.
OPPOSITE. The tree-climbing marten is frequently seen
in Yellowstone.

The long-tailed weasel, active both during the day and at night, prefers meadows and other open areas.

The mostly nocturnal mink makes a daytime appearance
with prey.

A badger drinking water is a common sight in the Lamar
Valley and near Mammoth Hot Springs.

ABOVE. River otters on the Gardner River.
PAGES 174–75. A leaping mountain lion.

ABOVE. The bobcat, which occupies the same habitat as
the lynx, is rarely seen in Yellowstone
OPPOSITE. Visitors seldom see the furtive lynx in the park.

Rocky Mountain cow elk with calves.

A Rocky Mountain bull elk can weigh as much as a thousand pounds (450 kg); the antlers of an animal in its prime weigh more than forty pounds (18 kg).

A mule deer doe.

Mule deer range widely throughout the park.

ABOVE. A bull moose, shown here with its antlers still in
summer velvet, is the second largest animal in the park,
after the bison.

OPPOSITE. Cow and calf moose nuzzling.

Pronghorn herds often gather near the park's
north entrance.

The pronghorn—North America's fastest land animal—can reach speeds of seventy miles an hour (110 kmph).

Bison calves.

Bison are one of the highlights of a drive through the Hayden Valley.

Bighorn sheep rams may be observed on the slopes
of Mount Washburn.

Bighorn sheep butt heads near the beginning of the fall
rutting season.

Above. Female red-necked grebe feeds a leech to her chick.
Pages 190–91. The common loon and a day-old chick.

May and June are the best months to see white pelicans in Yellowstone, while June, July, and October are prime viewing times for Barrow's goldeneyes, shown here in the foreground.

ABOVE. Canada geese frequent the park.
PAGES 194–95. Their distinctive call and appearance make it likely that trumpeter swans will be noticed by visitors.

Green-winged teals can be found on land, but marshes and mud flats are their usual haunts.

Female mallard.

Mallard chicks.

ABOVE. Barrow's goldeneye is abundant in the park.
OPPOSITE. The red-breasted merganser frequents clear
lakes and rivers.

Above. Ospreys perch together.
Opposite. Bald eagles survey the countryside from the tops
of pines and cottonwoods.

A female northern goshawk on a nest with eggs.

A peregrine falcon bathing.

A blue grouse displaying in spring.

A ruffed grouse displaying.

ABOVE. Coots nest in marshes, wetlands, or near lakes
or ponds, and dive to feed.
OPPOSITE. Sandhill cranes, although not widespread in the
park, can be seen from the roadside along Fountain Flat
Drive in the Lower Geyser Basin and along the Swan Lake
Flats south of Mammoth Hot Springs.

ABOVE. A robin-size killdeer on eggs.
OPPOSITE. The California gull is abundant in summer.

ABOVE. The great horned owl is distinguished by its ear tufts.
OPPOSITE. A female great gray owl with owlet on a nest.
This elusive bird of prey, the largest North American owl,
may be seen in meadows south of Canyon Village.

ABOVE. May, June, and July are the best months to observe
the timid Williamson's sapsucker.
OPPOSITE. Like other woodpeckers, the hairy woodpecker
hammers holes through bark, then pulls out grubs with
its long tongue.

The gray jay, common in Yellowstone year round, lives in forested areas, especially in stands of lodgepole pine.

Steller's jay—the only western jay with a crest.

Clark's nutcracker is abundant in the park.

Hundreds of mountain bluebirds nest in Yellowstone.

Above. A western meadowlark alongside lupine.
Opposite. A yellow-headed blackbird perched in tall grass.

Although an uncommon visitor to the park, the pine grosbeak may occasionally be glimpsed in any month.

Red crossbills, which breed in the park, are most likely to be
observed in June and July.

PLANTS

Despite an average elevation of more than 7,000 feet (2,100 m), a low mean annual temperature of about 33°F (1°C) and a growing season of just sixty frost-free days, Yellowstone supports more than one thousand species of plants in its diverse habitats.

About 80 percent of Yellowstone is forested, and 80 percent of its woodland is dominated by one tree species—the lodgepole pine, which thrives in the park's coarse soil. Mixed in with the lodgepoles are stands of quaking aspen. On higher slopes—about 8,000 feet (2,400 m) or so—Englemann spruce and subalpine fir mix with the lodgepoles. Gnarled white-bark pines survive on all but a few of the park's highest peaks. Here, too, and higher are the tenacious lichens, grasses, and tiny flowering plants of the alpine tundra. In July and early August, the tundra blooms with alpine asters, mountain bluebells, sky pilots, and phlox.

Subalpine fir is the most widely distributed fir in the West.

Bunchberry in August bloom, the Gibbon Meadow area.

The park's appearance was dramatically altered in places during the summer of 1988 when high winds whipped intense fires across 1.4 million acres (5,700 km²) of Yellowstone, more than half the park. Eight huge fires burned, but with varying degrees of intensity; much of the burn was relatively light. Only 20 percent of the park was affected by canopy fire. The Grand Canyon largely escaped the flames. Hayden Valley, with its rich diversity of birds and animals, escaped entirely. The resulting pattern was described as a mosaic. The worst areas of visual impact for visitors include the road from West Yellowstone to the Madison Junction and the road between Canyon Village and Norris Junction.

Seven years of regeneration has healed many of the blackened scars. Burned meadows recovered within a year. Burned forest floors were overgrown with ground cover in three to five years. Long dormant plants bloomed. Aspen, shrubs and other flora began to flourish in the greater sunlight and reduced competition in burned areas, providing increased forage for elk, bear, bison, moose, deer, and sheep. Bluebirds, woodpeckers, and other bird species also benefited from additional open areas, especially in productive zones along the borders of meadows and woods.

ABOVE AND OPPOSITE. Subalpine fir has a distinctive spirelike crown.

ABOVE AND OPPOSITE. Engelmann spruce, which has flexible, sharp needles, often grows in shady ravines.

ABOVE. The seeds of whitebark pines are a favorite
food of Clark's nutcracker.
OPPOSITE. White spruce grows in association with
black spruce in widespread forests, and is stunted to
shrub size at the tree line.

Lodgepole pine is the most common tree in Yellowstone.

Flexible twigs give the limber lodgepole pine its name.

ABOVE AND OPPOSITE. The distinctive seed pods of the
Douglas fir hang down, unlike those of true firs.

Rocky Mountain juniper grows near Mammoth
Hot Springs.

The quaking aspen's delicate leaves flutter in the
lightest breezes.

The Rocky Mountain maple flourishes near Mammoth Hot Springs.

In autumn the leaves of the Rocky Mountain maple turn brilliant red or yellow.

Spreading dogbane, a bushy plant, grows to a height of
about two feet (.6 m).

Yarrow has small, beautiful clusters of white flowers.

ABOVE. Pearly everlasting blooms for several weeks—hence
its name.
OPPOSITE. In Yellowstone, heartleaf arnica produces flowers
from June through mid-July.

Above. Arrowleaf balsam root is a favorite food of deer and elk.
Opposite. Alpine aster grows at high altitudes in rock crevices.

Wildlife feeds on the seeds and foliage of rabbit brush,
which grows in sagebrush areas.

Daisy fleabane.

ABOVE. Golden yarrow.
OPPOSITE. Prairie coneflower, a recent arrival to the park.

ABOVE. White-rayed mule's ear, a close relative of mule's ear, blooms in wet meadows.
OPPOSITE. Mule's ear is named for the shape of its long, shiny leaves.

The comb draba flourishes on open slopes throughout
the West.

Plains prickly pear, which grows in the Mammoth Hot
Springs area, is one of two cactus species in Yellowstone. 255

Above. As its name suggests, the Rocky Mountain bee plant
produces abundant nectar and lures bees.
Opposite. Showy mountain bluebells inhabit subalpine
meadows, particularly along streams.

Field chickweed.

Silene.

ABOVE. Indians called bearberry "kinnikinick," an expression that refers to the use of the species' bark and leaves with, or in place of, tobacco.
OPPOSITE. Fields of lupine brighten the park's meadows in summer.

Mountain thermopsis occupies wet meadows and
blossoms in summer.

The sticky geranium blooms from late spring through
August in sagebrush and open woods.

ABOVE. Ballhead waterleaf may be found in open woods
and shrubby areas.
OPPOSITE. Silky phacelia flowers in July and early August.

Above. The common selfheal was thought to have medicinal value.
Opposite. Glacier lilies blossom abundantly as soon as the snow melts.

ABOVE. The yellow bell's flowers become reddish or purplish as they age. The plant is found in the Hayden Valley and Dunraven Pass from May through June.
OPPOSITE. False Solomon's seal bears clusters of tiny white flowers.

ABOVE. The delicate flowers of wild blue flax open for only a
few hours in the afternoon.
OPPOSITE. Starry Solomon's seal.

ABOVE.The large pink flowers of globemallow are seen along
streams and roadsides from Mammoth Hot Springs south
to Teton Pass in July and August.

272

OPPOSITE. Scarlet globemallow.

Fireweed grows readily in burned and logged areas.

Red willowherb, a kind of evening primrose, blossoms from
late July to early September.

Above. The beautiful calypso orchid, one of Yellowstone's treasures, can be found in cool, deeply shaded areas for the first three weeks in June.
Opposite. Another orchid, the spotted coral root, grows in stands of lodgepole pine.

ABOVE. Look for ladies' tresses in thermal areas and
meadows from August to September.
OPPOSITE. Broomrape.

Narrowleaf collomia.

Tufted phlox is frequently seen in open pine woods.

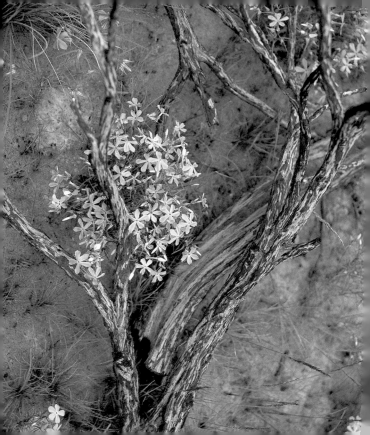

ABOVE. Sky pilot, or polemonium, spreads patches of blue
among the rocks of glacial moraines in July and August.
OPPOSITE. Phlox.

The delicate spring beauty flowers as soon as the snow melts.

Bitterroot, Montana's state flower.

The slimpod shooting star grows in sagebrush plains as well as wet mountain meadows.

Columbian monkshood also inhabits wet meadows and the
banks of streams in high mountain areas.

ABOVE. The graceful blue columbine, Colorado's state
flower, ornaments the park during July and August.
OPPOSITE. Look for hairy clematis in late June.

289

ABOVE. Buttercup.
OPPOSITE. Montana larkspur.

The sweet, juicy fruit of the western serviceberry sustains songbirds, as well as chipmunks, squirrels, and even bears.

White mountain avens often grows in large patches.

Globeflower blooms soon after the snow melts, especially in
boggy areas of the Beartooth Mountains.

Both birds and mammals feed on the fruit of the
beautiful wild rose.

ABOVE. Thimbleberry flourishes along shady streams.
and this is the second line
OPPOSITE. Spirea.

Indian paintbrush is Wyoming's state flower.

Butter-and-eggs closely resembles the cultivated
snapdragon.

ABOVE. The upper lip of the elephanthead corolla curves
upward and the two petals of the lower lip are shaped like
ears—hence the plant's name.
OPPOSITE. Lewis monkeyflower is a delightful discovery
along high canyon trails from 7,000 to 9,000 feet
(2,100–2,700 m).

ABOVE. Mountain penstemon, also known as beardstongue, is found in open, dry, and rocky areas in the park.
OPPOSITE. Look for the lovely Canada violet in moist woodlands from late June to early July.

TRAVEL TIPS

More than half of the park's 3 million annual visitors arrive in July and August, prime time for auto touring, viewing wildlife and thermal features, hiking, boating, and fishing. To avoid traffic and see more wildlife in summer, travel the major roadways before 10:30 a.m. and after 4:00 p.m.

Those who prefer to avoid crowds come in May and September and early October when the weather is good, visitors are few and wildlife is still abundant. Weather in May and June, however, may be cold, wet, even snowy.

An average of four feet (1.2 m) of snow blankets the park during the winter season, from mid-December to mid-March, when Yellowstone is open but facilities are limited. Only the road between the North and Northeast Entrances is open to cars. The other entrances are open only to over-the-snow vehicles.

The closest airports are at West Yellowstone (summer only), Bozeman, and Billings in Montana; and at Cody and Jackson in Wyoming.

There are five entrances to the park. In Montana,

US Highway 20 leads from the town of West Yellowstone to the West Entrance, US Highway 89 goes from Gardiner to the North Entrance, and US Highway 212 heads southwest from Cooke City to the Northeast Entrance. In Wyoming, US Highway 14/16/20 from Cody goes to the East Entrance and US Highway 89/191/287 leads to the South Entrance.

Visiting Yellowstone National Park

Address   Yellowstone National Park
P.O. Box 168
Wyoming 82190
(307) 344-7381

Visitor Centers

National Park Service visitor centers are located throughout Yellowstone at Mammoth Hot Springs (also the site of Park Headquarters), Canyon Village, Old Faithful, Fishing Bridge, and Grant Village. The centers are open from 8:00 a.m. to 7:00 p.m. (or later) in summer. Most interpretive activities begin mid-June and run through late August. Before and after these dates, activities occur mostly at Old Faithful, where exhibits at the visitor center explain and predict geyser eruptions. The Albright Museum and Visitor Center at Mammoth, open year round, contains a display of the region's human and natural history, Thomas Moran's watercolors, and William Henry Jackson's photographs from the 1871 Hayden expedition.

Park Fees

A $10-per-week fee for motorized vehicles is good for multiple entries at both Yellowstone and Grand Teton. Visitors arriving by foot, bicycle, or bus are charged $4.

Facilities for the Disabled

Visitor centers, Fishing Bridge RV Park and Madison Campground, most rest rooms, amphitheaters, many ranger-led activities, walks, and exhibits are wheelchair accessible. A free brochure itemizing facilities for the disabled is available from visitor centers and by writing Park Headquarters.

Accommodations

The park's nine commercial roofed facilities, which are usually open from June to September, are operated by TW Recreational Services,

Yellowstone National Park, Wyoming 82190. Call (307) 344-7311 for reservations at Canyon Lodge (572 cabins, restaurant); Grant Village (299 rooms, restaurant); Lake Lodge and Cabins (186 cabins, restaurant); Lake Yellowstone Hotel and Cabins (296 units, restaurants); Mammoth Hot Springs Hotel and Cabins (126 cabins, restaurant; hotel reopens from late December to early March); Old Faithful Inn (317 rooms, restaurant; open early May to mid-October); Old Faithful Lodge and Cabins (130 cabins, restaurant); Old Faithful Snow Lodge and Cabins (10 cabins, 30 rooms, restaurant; open mid-May to November and mid-December to mid-March); Roosevelt Lodge and Cabins (78 cabins, restaurant).

Campgrounds

Thirteen campgrounds have a 7-day limit from June 16 to August 25; at other times of year the maximum stay is 30 days. The Mammoth Campground is open year round; the rest are open late spring to mid-autumn. For reservations at Fishing Bridge RV Park, contact TW Recreational Services. For reservations at Bridge Bay from mid-June to early September, call Ticketron at (213) 410-

1720, (303) 825-8447, or (602) 340-9033. All other campgrounds are first come, first served. Most campgrounds offer tent and RV sites, but there are only RV sites at Canyon, Fishing Bridge, and Fishing Bridge RV Park. For camping information, call (307) 344-2114 (summer only).

Camping and Picnic Supplies

Camping supplies as well as picnic items are available at the Hamilton Stores, a concession located throughout the park. Staff at the Lake Hotel pack picnic lunches if the request is made the night before by dinnertime.

Outdoor Activities

Short Itineraries

A complete road tour of Yellowstone, taking in the major features (Mammoth Hot Springs, the Grand Canyon of the Yellowstone, and Old Faithful) requires three full days. If your itinerary allows only a one-day visit to Yellowstone, stop at a visitor center, develop your strategy with a park interpretive officer, then set out on the Grand Loop Road, which passes major points of interest and virtually guarantees wildlife sightings. Although the speed limit in the park is 45 m.p.h. (72 kmph), expect to average 25 m.p.h. (40 kmph) in summer on the 142-mile (227 km) circuit. That means the Grand Loop takes about 5½ hours to drive.

If you'd rather spend less time behind the wheel and more time appreciating nature, choose either the Upper Loop or the Lower Loop of the figure eight. You can increase your amount of sightseeing by selecting the loop closest to your park entrance or accommodation within the park. If you're based in Cody, for example, it's more efficient to drive the Lower Loop. Those who seek solitude visit the northern part of the park in general and the lightly traveled northeastern corner in particular.

An itinerary for a long weekend affords enough time for traveling the Upper Loop one day and the Lower Loop the next. You'll also be able to get out of the car and take Yellowstone more on its own terms along a boardwalk or nature trail. People of all ages enjoy the hike up Mount Washburn, the hike to Fairy Falls in the

Firehole River area, and the hike to Storm Point on Yellowstone Lake.

Wildlife Viewing

Morning and late afternoon are the best times for wildlife viewing, since most of the park's animals are nocturnal or crepuscular (active at dawn and dusk). Even at midday, however, areas such as the Hayden Valley are likely to provide sightings of large mammals and birds.

The most popular activity for car-bound visitors is enhanced by binoculars and viewing scopes. Here are some of the prime areas.

Hayden Valley

The Hayden Valley, dissected by the Yellowstone River, is the park's premier wildlife viewing area. The open meadows offer superb grazing for elk, bison, and grizzlies, and the wetlands provide excellent habitat for white pelicans, bald eagles, and trumpeter swans. A number of pullouts offer good viewing points and roadside interpretive displays.

Yellowstone Lake

The northern shore of Yellowstone Lake between Fishing Bridge and Steamboat Point is frequented by river otters, mule deer, and moose. Just south of Bridge Bay, the shoreline Gull Point Drive is a good place to look for California gulls, Barrow's goldeneyes, belted kingfishers, lesser scaups, buffleheads, common snipes, and spotted sandpipers.

Lamar Valley

The more remote Lamar Valley in the northeastern corner of the park is home to elk, bison, mule deer, coyotes, badgers, mountain lions, redtailed hawks, and golden and bald eagles.

Gardners Hole

Another good viewing area is at Gardners Hole in the northwestern corner of the park, where moose, elk, white-tailed deer, trumpeter swans, coyotes, and the occasional grizzly frequent the marshy banks of Beaver Ponds, Obsidian Creek, and Indian Creek. Stands of willow along Obsidian Creek also provide good habitat for Wilson's warblers, yellow warblers, and other songbirds. In the surrounding pine forest are yellow-rumped warblers, dark-eyed juncos, and red-breasted nuthatches. To the north, Willow Valley between Apollinaris Spring and Indian Creek Campground is great moose country in summer.

Mammoth Hot Springs

A herd of elk resides in the Mammoth Hot Springs area. From Mammoth north to the park boundary, pronghorns are often seen on sagebrush flats; look for bighorn sheep along clifftops.

Tower and Mount Washburn Areas

Bighorns are also seen in the Tower Fall and Mount Washburn areas (depending on the altitude of the remaining snowpack); hikers often encounter these sheep along the Chittenden Road on the north side of Washburn. Bears generally keep to the backcountry, but with luck they can be seen on the hillsides or in the valley of Antelope Creek north of Mount Washburn.

Gibbon Meadows and Firehole River

Elk and bison can usually be seen in Gibbon Meadows near the Norris Geyser Basin and at Fountain Flats. These two species use forest meadows as calving grounds along the Firehole River between the Upper Geyser Basin and the Madison River. Look for bison calves in May, elk calves in June. Grizzlies and sandhill cranes are also found along the Firehole.

Hiking

More than twelve hundred miles (1,920 km) of trails wind through the park. A popular day outing is the three-mile (4.8 km) walk from Dunraven Pass up to the lookout on Mount Washburn. On a clear day, you can see the Tetons 100 miles (160 km) south, the outline of the caldera, and other geologic features. Bighorn sheep are often encountered along the way.

Interesting hikes in the Grand Canyon of the Yellowstone include the Red Rock Point Hike from the North Rim down to the Lower Falls; the challenging hike to the Brink of the Lower Falls, which ends where the powerful cascade shoots over a resistant rock ledge; and the even more difficult Uncle Tom's Trail on the South Rim to the Lower Falls.

In the Old Faithful area, a short hike takes you away from the crowds to Observation Point and Solitary Geyser. Just south of Old Faithful, a six-mile (9.6 km) trail along the Firehole River goes to Lone Star Geyser. North, a mile-long (1.6 km) trail at the Biscuit Basin follows the Little Firehole River to enchanting Mystic Falls.

The three best backcountry hiking areas are the Bechler country in the southwest, also known as Cascade Corner for its abundant waterfalls; the Hoodoo Basin in the northeast, with the rugged badlands sculpture of the Absarokas; and the Snake River region in the south and east to the Thorofare country. Backcountry permits are required for overnight trips.

Swimming

Lake waters are generally too cold for swimming. It is illegal and dangerous to swim in any of the park's thermal features. That still leaves a few options, however. Perhaps the most interesting place to swim is in the Firehole River in Firehole Canyon, where the geothermally heated waters reach up to 80°F (27°C) in summer—very warm for the northern Rockies. Some swimmers ride white-water riffles through one section of the gorge.

Just south of the North Entrance, an undeveloped hot spring known as the Boiling River flows over rocks alongside the Gardner River, where swimmers have created soaking pools by moving rocks to the pool's edges. Turn into the parking area at the sign marked "45th Parallel." The soaking pools are a quarter mile upriver (no facilities).

Fishing

General William Tecumseh Sherman pronounced the Yellowstone River "the best trout-fishing stream on earth." Other park rivers and Yellowstone Lake are also renowned for their cutthroat trout. Most roadside streams, easily accessible, are catch-and-release only. On some streams fly-fishing only is permitted. Various limits and restrictions apply. Fishing permits are required.

Boating

Scenic cruises, charters, boat rentals, marine supplies, and ranger services are all available at the Bridge Bay Marina on Yellowstone Lake. Boat ramps are at Bridge Bay and Grant Village Campground on Yellowstone Lake, and at Lewis Lake. All boats must have a permit, available from the Bridge Bay Marina or at park ranger stations in the lake district. Boats, canoes, kayaks, and rafts are not allowed on park rivers and streams.

Horseback Riding

Trail rides are available from corrals at Canyon, Roosevelt, and Mammoth.

Winter Activities

Staff at the Mammoth Hot Springs Hotel and the
Old Faithful Snow Lodge (the only park accommodations open in winter) provide information
about shuttles to and from cross-country skiing
trails, snowcoach tours, and snowmobile rentals.
More than forty miles (64 km) of cross-country
trails wind through the Old Faithful area, including the Biscuit Basin Loop Trail from the Snow
Lodge to Old Faithful Geyser. Short trails are also
located on the Blacktail Deer Plateau, in the
Lamar Valley and along the lower reaches of Specimen Ridge. The Lower Loop and parts of the
Upper Loop are groomed for snowmobile traffic.

Wildlife Viewing

Location Key

AC	Antelope Creek	LV	Lamar Valley
FR	Firehole River	MHSA	Mammoth Hot Springs Area
FF	Fountain Flats		
GH	Gardners Hole	MW	Mount Washburn
GM	Gibbon Meadows	WV	Willow Valley
HV	Hayden Valley	YLNS	Yellowstone Lake North Shore

Mammals

- ☐ Bison HV, LV, FF, GM, FR
- ☐ Coyote LV, GH
- ☐ Deer, Mule YLNS, LV
- ☐ Deer, White-tailed GH
- ☐ Elk HV, LV, FF, GM, FR, GH, MHSA
- ☐ Grizzly HV, GH, AC
- ☐ Moose YLNS, WV, GH
- ☐ Mountain lion LV
- ☐ River otter HV, YLNS
- ☐ Pronghorn MHSA
- ☐ Bighorn sheep MHSA, MW

Birds

- ☐ Bufflehead YLNS
- ☐ Sandhill crane FR
- ☐ Eagle, Bald HV, LV
- ☐ Eagle, Golden LV
- ☐ Barrow's goldeneye YLNS
- ☐ California gull YLNS
- ☐ Red-tailed hawk LV
- ☐ Dark-eyed junco GH
- ☐ Belted kingfisher YLNS
- ☐ Red-breasted nuthatch GH
- ☐ White pelican HV
- ☐ Spotted sandpiper YLNS
- ☐ Lesser scaup YLNS
- ☐ Common snipe YLNS
- ☐ Lincoln's sparrow GH
- ☐ Trumpeter swan HV, LV
- ☐ Warbler, Wilson's GH
- ☐ Warbler, Yellow GH
- ☐ Warbler, Yellow-rumped GH

PARK CONSERVATION

The first national parks were created out of a sense of cultural identity, as a way to take pride in something uniquely American. Since then, citizens have played an active role in park protection, speaking out on behalf of sound park management; monitoring inappropriate use of parklands; identifying adjacent land activities threatening park resources; and publicizing those issues to park personnel, the media, and the public. Local action has always been critical to park protection. Here are some basic ways to take action at your park and to understand its needs.

How much time can you spare?

A Few Hours a Month

Read and Research

Park-related issues and stories are at the forefront of the environmental movement. Activists must first educate themselves on park issues before they can begin the process of educating others.

Join a local or national park advocacy organization

Park groups rely on active membership bases to support programs, fund educational materials, and to increase the visibility of park issues among the media, elected officials, the Park Service, and the general public. Most groups provide their members with newsletters or magazines that are good primers for understanding specific park issues and suggestions to take in response. Local park advocacy groups have smaller memberships and fewer resources than their counterparts at the national level. National park advocacy groups involve their members in special activist corps by recruiting them to work on key park issues at the local level.

Write letters and make phone calls

Raise the level of awareness of your elected officials and park issues by writing or phoning them for their position. This will let them know that their constituents care about the problems facing national parks and are interested in how government works to solve these problems. An informed constituency creates a heightened response to park problems.

One Day a Month

Attend the meeting of your local park group

These meetings provide an important way to meet with other park activists. It's also a good way to let others know you want to do something for your park.

Get on the park mailing list

Parks maintain mailing lists of citizens who want to be informed of any management actions. Ask to be placed on the list for your parks and stress that you want to be notified of any opportunities to participate in "scoping." (Scoping is an agency's solicitation of public opinion on an action.)

Go visit your park

Become familiar with your park so that you are able to notice when the park is being improved, neglected, or altered in any way. When you do notice a problem, be sure to alert the park. Either write to the superintendent and ask for a response, or call and ask for the person who handles the type of problem you are reporting. Also alert your local and national advocacy groups.

Write a letter to the editor for your local newspaper

The news media are important in raising the visibility of park issues.

A Few Days a Month or More

Volunteer

To do volunteer work, contact your park directly or contact the National Park Service interpretation division at (202) 619-7077 and ask for information on becoming a volunteer.

Develop relationships with the park staff

Become familiar with your park's staff and their duties.

Participate in park planning

National Park Service (NPS) policies require public involvement. The general management plan is the comprehensive plan for your park and should be guiding decisions made by NPS staff. Become familiar with this document so that you have a point of reference for any activity occurring in the park. Make sure you are on the park mailing list. Activists should offer comments on all park management plans.

Build a network of people in your community interested in protecting your park

If there is a park advocacy group in your area, be an active member and help recruit interested local community members (contact NPCA for a park advocacy group in your area). Seek to develop a well-rounded coalition that represents all aspects of the community.

Your involvement in protecting national parks becomes more important every day. As development pressures make open space increasingly scarce, ecosystems and wildlife habitat that depend on parks and their adjacent lands are being destroyed at a growing rate. America's cultural heritage is being paved over to build suburban shopping malls. Park budgets are being cut at an even faster rate. The battle to protect our national parks is a continuing challenge. A committed, vocal community of park supporters is key to winning the battle.

The National Parks and Conservation Association (NPCA) is America's only private nonprofit citizen organization dedicated solely to protecting, preserving, and enhancing the U.S. National Park System. Founded in 1919 as an association of "Citizens Protecting America's Parks," NPCA has 450,000 members.

To become a member of NPCA, send a tax-deductible membership contribution of $25 to: NPCA, 1776 Massachusetts Avenue, N.W., Washington, DC 20036. Members receive *National Parks,* an award-winning bimonthly magazine.

INDEX

INDEX

All photographs are by Jerry Pavia except those on the following pages: Michael H. Francis: 152, 176, 186, 200, 202, 218; © Tom and Pat Leeson: 146, 148, 151, 154–56, 158–61, 165–67, 173–75, 183, 185, 188–89, 212, 220; © Tom Mangelson: 180; © Larry Mayer: 28–9, 54, 55, 72, 95, 96, 127, 128; © Sandy Nykerk: 153, 162–63; Michael Quinton: 150, 157, 164, 168–72, 177, 182, 190–93, 197, 201, 203–11, 213–17, 219, 222–23.